*Come the Slumberless to the
Land of Nod*

Come the Slumberless to the Land of Nod

Traci Brimhall

COPPER CANYON PRESS
PORT TOWNSEND, WASHINGTON

Cover art: Jason deCaires Taylor, *Vicissitudes,* 2007. © Jason deCaires Taylor.
All rights reserved, DACS / ARS 2019

Copper Canyon Press is in residence at Fort Worden State Park
in Port Townsend, Washington, under the auspices of Centrum.
Centrum is a gathering place for artists and creative thinkers
from around the world, students of all ages and backgrounds,
and audiences seeking extraordinary cultural enrichment.

LIBRARY OF CONGRESS CATALOGING-IN-PUBLICATION DATA
Names: Brimhall, Traci, 1982– author.
Title: Come the slumberless to the land of nod / Traci Brimhall.
Description: Port Townsend : Copper Canyon Press, [2020] |
Identifiers: LCCN 2019043454 | ISBN 9781556595806 (trade paperback)
Subjects: LCGFT: Poetry.
Classification: LCC PS3602.R53177 C66 2020 | DDC 811/.6—dc23
LC record available at https://lccn.loc.gov/2019043454

98765432 FIRST PRINTING

COPPER CANYON PRESS
Post Office Box 271
Port Townsend, Washington 98368
www.coppercanyonpress.org

Acknowledgments

Many thanks to the editors of the following publications where these poems and essays first appeared, sometimes in earlier versions:

The American Poetry Review, The Baffler, Blackbird, Black Tongue Review, BuzzFeed Reader, Colorado Review, Copper Nickel, Crazyhorse, Field, Guernica, Gulf Coast, The Los Angeles Review, The Missouri Review, Narrative, New England Review, The New Yorker, Ninth Letter, Orion, Oxford American, Phantom Limb, Ploughshares, Poet Lore, Poetry Northwest, Raleigh Review, 32 Poems, TriQuarterly, Virginia Quarterly Review, and *West Branch.*

"Bedtime Story with *Goodnight Moon* & CNN" appeared as "Still Life with Rocking Chair, *Goodnight Moon* and CNN" in the anthology *Still Life with Poem,* edited by Jehanne Dubrow and Lindsay Lusby.

"Bedtime Story with *Goodnight Moon* & CNN" was also reprinted by *Love's Executive Order.*

"Dear Thanatos, [I did what you told me . . .]" was selected by Denise Duhamel for *The Best American Poetry 2013.*

"Fledgling" first appeared in the Poem-a-Day series from the Academy of American Poets.

"Fledgling" also appeared in the anthology *Here: Poems for the Planet,* edited by Elizabeth J. Coleman.

"How to Write a Love Poem" was reprinted as a chapbook by Thrush Press.

"Kything" was reprinted in the 2018 *Orison Anthology,* edited by Luke Hankins, Nathan Poole, and Karen Tucker.

"Murder Ballad in the Arctic" was selected by Leslie Jamison as a notable essay for *The Best American Essays 2017*.

Thanks to those who read this book and pushed it forward:
Jenny Molberg, Jennifer Militello, Tomás Q. Morín, John Murillo.

And thank you to the amazing team at Copper Canyon:
Michael Wiegers, Emily Grise, Janeen Armstrong, Laura Buccieri, John Pierce, Joseph Bednarik, and George Knotek.

Thanks also to copyeditors Alison Lockhart and Jessica Roeder.
But most of all, thanks to my incredible editor, Elaina Ellis,
for her incisive eye and tireless support.
Thank you for helping this book become its best self.

For Vince, forgive me for not answering

For Elliot, every other love is prose

Thare iz no revenge so komplete az forgivness.

JOSH BILLINGS

None of the characters in these songs ever show their face. It is essential that they move on, opening the way to places where the water is deeper and the bird has forever renounced its wings.

FEDERICO GARCÍA LORCA, "ON LULLABIES"

Contents

Come the Slumberless to the
Land of Nod

Dear Thanatos,

I am three thoughts away from the grave,
two steps away from the open door,
one kiss away from the bridge.

Dear volcano, where are you?
Dear battleship, your warplanes

sit on the bottom of the sea,
eels coiled in the cockpits.
Dear moon, you were an accident.

Dear heart, you birdcage left at low tide,
what's living in you is dark and songless.

Dear ghost, I don't have your forgiveness.
Leave my attic, crawl down the drainpipe
to slumberless tunnels beneath the city.

Wet ashes were once commandments,
vigilant and unforgiving.

Dear garden, I promise I still wander.
Dear fossil, I am sorry for the light.

Family Portrait as Lullaby

Your father is the slow dance, and I am the ballad.
Or he's the nightclub, and I am six tequila shots on the bar.
I am the salt and lemon, too.

I am the snake and the apple. I am the tongue that says
to your father—*Take. Eat. Do this in remembrance of*—
Your father, the monologue in the music box
and I, the plastic ballerina, the golden shoes.

Your father is the swaddle, the rock, the cradle.
His potbellied heart loses its socks.
My heart, a boondocks opera.

You are Mars. Your father and I are its two moons orbiting.
You, stardust on the telescope's lens,
the ice in the comet's tail.

Your heart is a poppy—bright, forgetful.
You are the first mayapple of spring, unripe and rising.
And this is the hallelujah I asked the first star
to sing at the quickening.

This is the dirty Eden, stalked by envious angels.
This is the land of Isaac, and of knives.

We are the wish imperfectly granted, and this is the well.

Self-Deliverance

Can I say it? I am of a darker nature, one that might ask
a man to do something worth repenting. Say, a whip.

A harness. Say, pleasure any way I want it. I want a body
with another body to say more than words. The light

furrowing of nails on shoulder blades to signify *you*
and *forever* and *yes*. A hand on a breast to signify: *I want*

you like a pious woman wants God's middle finger to scrape
the psalm from her tongue. The child I carry turns in the dark

of its first loneliness, thumb in its mouth, learning
what it must. I'd like to think that love for one kills desire

for all others. I'd like to think my doubts prove I hunger
for the eternal, but I am wet and Sapphic like any good

sinner, all sad cry and gentle astonishment that a body
with another body burns brief and desperate as prayer.

Lullaby on Mount Moriah

The lullaby I wrote on your throat about the stained
hilt of the knife in my hand begins—*Whisper, or snow
will come and make its sadness famous in your mouth.*

The why of you a radiant devilfish, the what of you
a fat little soul bluing at the edges.

The surest way to receive a free ram is to tie your son's hands
behind his back. *Offer me a metaphor,* God said.
Abraham stretched Isaac out on a rock, *Like this?*

Don't be impatient with the gift. It will bleed out in the time
it takes shadows and atoms to inch their way between stars.

Every fire thinks it's a part of God, but lightning
is not a promise, a flag is not a shield. Love wants you
to believe that there's a God somewhere who can

do your dying for you. There are raptures that won't
come for you and raptures that will.

In between, satellites blink the news to the lights in our hands.
Love will teach you many things, most of them tragic—

like last kisses and letters under your windshield wipers,
like helplessness, like the man on the news weeping
and carrying what remains of his son in a plastic bag.

And Abraham said, *This is how much I love you,* and measured
Isaac from ankle to scalp. Love will gut you and then ask

you to carry on singing with light on your tongue
as a father finds flies crowning his son's dreamless head,
lambent as the hand of God ushering a late ram from the bushes.

Bedtime Story with *Goodnight Moon* & CNN

Here, the now turns the cardboard pages to telephones
and red balloons. *Goodnight moon. Goodnight room.*

There in the then, a scarecrow stuffed with a missing
woman's hair. There on the ground, a wolf spider

with a September hunger and blind in half her eyes.
Back, back in your newest hour, a woman vanished

and no one looked for her. Dark, dark my stalk and tassel.
Darker still my shadow's voice reciting newborn gospels,

ardent as the sing and saw of wind. *Goodnight nobody.*
Goodnight mush. Rock, rock in a stippled field. Hush

as the rest of her is found in an abandoned building
with other bodies curled into positions of sleep or rapture.

Who knows how many we could find, the officer says as teams
sweep the empty blocks. *He wanted women no one would miss.*

This motive relieves me—I would miss your nose, your ears,
your sour breath; therefore you are safe. Emergency numbers

secure on the fridge, the reassurance of curtains. *Goodnight air.*
Goodnight noises everywhere. Soft, soft the windfall apples. Softer

still the curled fists gripping the yes of the world, the television's
cadence of tragedy and sleepless months revised into happiness,

the yes of flies corseting a body, the yes of night shepherding
shadows closer to home. Yes, the moon, the bright unending.

Love Poem without a Drop of Hyperbole

I love you like ladybugs love windowsills, love you
like sperm whales love squid. There's no depth

I wouldn't follow you through. I love you like
the pawns in chess love aristocratic horses.

I'll throw myself in front of a bishop or a queen
for you. Even a sentient castle. My love is crazy

like that. I like that sweet little hothouse mouth
you have. I like to kiss you with tongue, with gusto,

with socks still on. I love you like a vulture loves
the careless deer at the roadside. I want to get

all up in you. I love you like Isis loved Osiris,
but her devotion came up a few inches short.

I'll train my breath and learn to read sonar until
I retrieve every lost blood vessel of you. I swear

this love is ungodly, not an ounce of suffering in it.
Like salmon with its upstream itch, I'll dodge grizzlies

for you. Like hawks to skyscraper rooftops,
I'll keep coming back. Maddened. A little hopeless.

Embarrassingly in love. And that's why I'm on
the couch kissing pictures on my phone instead of

calling you in from the kitchen where you are
undoubtedly making dinner too spicy, but when

you hold the spoon to my lips and ask if it's ready
I'll say it is, always, but never, there is never enough.

Chthonic Lullaby

Hush, hush, sweet godling stirring underground.
Rush, rush, little sprite furling and unbound,
an inch of hair fuzzing your head. Empyrean,

your hunger hurts you awake. The sin is not
the wanting, it's the wanting more. Stars, perhaps,

unburnt in your pocket, innocent of any sensual crime,

charmed by rhyme to remember you in whichever
sea you swell. Swim, swim for the shore. Steer

by the bells. Sing, sing, for the nightingales refuse
to be governed. I sinned with conviction and dug
the grave for it with my bare hands. What saved me

was secular and let me paint it naked. Lullay, little
episteme, darling potential, possibility all radical, radiant.

Quick, quick, dreamling, unclench your fist and churn.

Sound waves turn sibilant, showing a future that might
be ours. And in the messianic tomorrow, a white horse.

And in the dialectic, pleasure and pain. And in the child,
a white shadow I praise until my sadness is paling
and perfect and tries to nurse from my fingers.

Cosmic Lullaby

Then your mouth draws in the night, eyelids thin
as onion skin twitch, and I know you're finally
in the dream that belongs to you alone, though

your fears may wear my face. I can't rescue you.
Cries bow your back like the hull of a boat that
might sail on a solar wind to a remote archipelago

of rogue planets, or to a star's nuclear birth, or a nova's
bombastic ending, or to the marbled Earth's tireless
revolutions in night vision's green static. All I can

do is rock you into a safety beyond my reach—
in the deepening spell of sleep, where you don't know
the news peeled back history's scabs to discover

Spanish priests stole thousands of newborns from
unwed girls and sold them. When each new mother cried
and asked to see her child, nuns had one on hand—

small and frozen, blue with an old death—that each
young woman held to her chest, weeping onto its
frosted forehead as it dreamed its permanent dream

of hide-and-seek with angels in catacombs, as its body
accepted the kisses and cries of a thousand mothers.
Even though they held the wrong baby, the grief

was as real and cold as the pounds in their hands.
Now the reporter tells them: *What you thought was lost
has been found and is studying medicine at a college in Texas!*

Phones come alive on walls, shrilling the air, and the love
those mothers felt when they held that cold dreamer
monsters awake with a need so bright it could be dawn.

Kything

Lord, there is nothing special about you,
unless bluestem is, unless the *seet, seet*
of the yellow warbler is a disobedient

prayer you always honor, unless the crows
hunched on the fencepost like a common row

of puritans haven't commanded me to dig
a grave with my hands like an animal and lie
in it, a guest. Too much. Too much breath.

Nothing here is special unless a grasshopper
graces it, unless the way cicadas bruise

the silence is dear to those who hear it.
The danger here is wind and the way
last year's grasses give themselves too

easily to the drip torch. Lord, I still grieve
the daughter I didn't want. Her blood

burned on the bathroom floor, her new
skyless life among root-lace. Pin of her heart
stitched into the living field, the bluest stone.

There is nothing special about her unless
grief is special to those who carry it. My God,

who knows what it is to lose a child, I lie
in the ground as if I'd made a burrow and not
a burial, as if all sleeps are hibernations, as if

all this weeping is waiting for the new season
to brighten the ground around me with snow.

Lullaby with Almost All the Answers

The bridesmaids in yellow silk harvesting pears
is when. Love set you going is why.

One-third of the spirit entering me is why.

Moonlight gentling the curtains is how.
The angel Gabriel is who. The husband is who.

The stranger next to me on the bus who let me

warm my hands on her thighs is who. We all want
to be broken for one another is why.

We all want to kiss our names from someone else's

mouth is why. The tongue is where. Neck is where.
Collarbone, nipple, and navel are where.

The amethyst hour is when. The dazzlement
of mosquitoes in bluelight is when.

Why: winter approached and heat was scarce

or the fourth glass of wine or old-fashioned loneliness.
My blood on the toothbrush is what. I wanted

a child to live long enough to call me mother is why.

Dear Eros,

I have found you where I shouldn't—in the wrong bodies,
at the wrong time, and once on a subway platform
with my feet stuck to a dried pool of soda, taking gum
from a near-stranger's mouth. That night you were spearmint
and the 6 train. I have been woken by you, put to bed by you.
Had you serve me coffee in my favorite mug with milk
and just enough sweetness. An easy gift. A debt of pleasure.
My therapist said: *Sometimes it's better to be understood than it is*
to be loved. I believed her because I am better at understanding
than I am at feeling. I have said *I love you* to men whose names
I can't remember now. And who's to say it wasn't true?
Who's to say I couldn't have tried forever with any of them?
Couldn't have tried learning to sail and opened a sanctuary
for elephants, or perfected the tambourine and followed
the band on their bluegrass tour? *I don't know why anyone stays*
in their marriage, my therapist said. *Love is illogical.* Once, a man
I loved raped me. I did not leave him. At least not then.
But the next time I loved, I chose someone kinder. I thought
it would make a difference. I stopped meeting people's eyes
when talking to them, because I couldn't stop wanting to
kiss them, the intimacy of language turning into metaphor
and urge. Everyone. I wanted to kiss the cashier handling
my poblanos with such gentleness and curiosity. To kiss
the person next to me on the bus with bad taste in music,
and vanilla and bergamot in his cologne. Kiss the woman
holding the door, saying: *Have a good day.* Her smile
so goddamn bright and real and meant for me.

You're trapped, my therapist tells me. *Only you can break*
this cycle. But I have sweat between my breasts that needs
licking. I have an iamb in my chest that keeps skipping.
I have stockings on my thighs. Oh, I've got stockings
on my thighs that need ripping. I read my way through
all the paperback romances and need a more adequate
fiction. I need my hair pulled, mean and gentle. I dressed
you up in every excuse and black gloves past the elbow.

You open the silk in me with zippers and buttons sewed
on with breakable thread. I have pulled tinsel from your hair
and called it mistletoe, led you into the woods wearing cheap
underwear and handed you the switchblade from my boot.
I worshipped the myth I made of you, but I'm off my knees
now. I want your hands to become language and make me
offer you one thigh at a time. Let it sting loud and sweetly.
Let bruise be the proof. Let the smell of your hands.

How to Write a Love Poem

Begin with blackbirds you shot for menacing
the finches. Begin with your suitcase full of maps.

Begin with the man who knocked on your door
and said the world was ending. He hung your sheets

on the line, gathered squash from the garden,
kissed you on the porch, but you wouldn't let him

save you. Don't begin with the black bear that came
down from the mountain to steal your goat.

Begin with the orange kite you fly each spring.
Begin with the cocoon that shakes in your hand

when you speak to it. Begin by telling someone
about the man who raped you and the woman who

helped hold you down. Begin with the deer you found
field dressed and hanging from the arbor gate,

mistletoe pinned to its cheek, a note tied around
its neck that read: *To help you survive the winter.*

Murder Ballad in the Arctic

He was little or nothing but life.
Virginia Woolf

In a fjord, the half-decomposed remains of a juvenile seal and the skeleton of a pup on its back. On the short cliffs, the bones of a bird I can't identify. I catalogue the dead I can name—puffin, narwhal, walrus. Near my foot, a fly, the only living thing. So rarely am I in a place that would kill me, and this one can in so many ways. Everyone here praises the landscape, tosses about *sublime* and *inspired* on the deck of the ship as they polish their camera lenses or write postcards home, but can't they see the rapture could pull our guts from our bellies with its beak, or club us on the head and leave us on a polar beach to rot? The wind is cold and incessant and everything in me wants to live.

———

I've come here looking for Nod—Cain's biblical place of exile and the drifting space of dream in lullabies. I thought the arctic summer, that region of never-night, might be a place I could write about my friend's murder and the child I'm carrying. I thought the ice cap could teach me what it might mean to wander as punishment for murder, or what dreams might look like to my son, who's never seen color and never known fear, but all I see is glacier, mountain, sea, glacier, mountain, sea, glaciermountainsea.

I haven't yet felt my son move, and even though I have a grainy sonogram as proof he is attached and unfurling, he is as abstract to me as God or death. I try to make him real by writing him lullabies, but they all end up being about loss or landscapes that won't put my child to sleep—cactuses used for target practice, bullet casings jingling like spurs in the tumbleweeds, the canyon roads I used to drive at night, rolling back the headlight switch to see how long I could travel that speed in the dark and remain alive.

———

In "On Lullabies," Federico García Lorca said: "Various crucial elements are involved in lulling the child to sleep, including, of course, the consent of the fairies. The fairies bring the windflowers and the right climate. The mother and the song supply the rest." I don't know what an arctic fairy might look like, though I imagine Cain's son with wings and a seal's spinal cord for a wand. Something made of magic and fear bearing purple saxifrage and a mild polar evening. In the lullaby I compose for my son, I write, *Before Socrates drank the hemlock, he washed his body to save his loved ones the trouble.* All my rhymes call to mind Macbeth's witches, which may be as close to Lorca's consenting fairies as I can get.

———

Someone pulls a sea angel out of the ocean and puts it in a jar on the deck of our ship. It is small and translucent, flapping its wings and turning slow circles in the glass. Angels are hermaphrodites. Lately, polar bears have been born with both sets of sex organs, too, but unlike the angels, hermaphroditic polar bears cannot reproduce. Like most things about this place, these animals make me think of an abstinent god, a bored sublimity. Oh, to be everything and unable to create.

I drop a sea butterfly, the angel's mollusk cousin, into the jar, and the angel's gentle flutter turns vicious. Its translucent mouth grows large, rapacious. Always the comfort of a quick and necessary death—to know our life could be snatched away in seconds, but it isn't. Instead, the seal. Instead, the snow bunting. Instead, the jellyfish dead against the rocks, as slick and purple as the ocean depths that gave it up.

———

My cabinmate on the ship, a visual artist, once investigated how women's murders were consistently reported to take place in beautiful locations. Often these "beauty spots" weren't that beautiful at all, but the newspapers used lyrical descriptions to heighten the romantic horror of the death. Somehow it made the story more scintillating—a picturesque location, a lovely woman, a murderer prowling the park benches with endearments and piano wire. My cabinmate says the "beauty spot" murders are even more sinister because a woman's body in nature is one of the tropes of pastoral poetry—the woman's body available for wooing and erotic encounter. I wonder if the newspaper reporters covering the discovery of these women's bodies thought of love poems as they drank their coffee, wrote their copy late into the night, and fantasized about their readers.

Perhaps I'm guilty of this same need to make death lovely. I've tried imagining my friend's murder to seem peaceful, a quick release. I've written about the location of his death with the same fetish for beauty. His body in a field, under stars, the saw grass rustling in the late spring breezes. I wonder if the song I'm writing for my son has Betelgeuse and Bellatrix, those dual spring stars, burning in it. If it has field and grass and wind. If it has wool and bell in it, or if it has a darker twin—a shadow under the water and three rows of teeth, or an ice field and empty pockets, or a highway in a car squeezed between two strangers who say they don't want to hurt you.

"A dead person is deader in Spain than anywhere else in the world. And whoever wants to leap into dream wounds their feet on the edge of a barber's razor," Lorca said, though he'd never been to the Arctic. Still, the icy water leaks through my boots and I lean into the beauty at dream's edge.

———

Minutes of silence and wind and rain and oblivion so goddamn still and needing nothing. Here, the oblivion is white and cold and has little to do with joy. I don't know what each artist and writer on the ship is learning about themselves, but we are all learning about the north—the names of its flowers, the dangers of its mating birds, the sound of glaciers preparing to calve. The wind won't quit, the rain joins it, and everyone is quietly photographing the shack of a trapper who lives there all year, alone.

———

In the new lullaby I write for my son, I want to teach him about the earth, not to "plunge the child fully into raw reality, imbuing it with the drama of the world," as Lorca suggested, but to teach him the rhythms of the trade winds, or how arctic terns travel from the Arctic to the Antarctic every year. How well they must know the oceans. How tireless they must be. I want to teach him how to fashion his own splint if he falls while hiking. I need him to know how to debride a wound.

———

All the books I read on the ship are about survival. There are how-to books about knots, advice on sailing, descriptions of how lost explorers traversed the pack ice. Sometimes the bones of sailors are found. Sometimes sheets of ice preserved their whole bodies, the dog hair still on their coats, the pictures of beloveds still in their pockets. There's no clear answer about how long a murderer could wander in this landscape if he were exiled here—days, weeks, months—though his chances for survival would improve if he were not alone. I look at the three mug shots and try to imagine who would make it the longest in exile. Who looks like he could bear the cold and rain and hunger and sublime loneliness of a banishment on ice? I decide it is the one whose name I once wanted to give my son.

———

We come across an ice floe and anchor the ship. Every artist takes turns walking across the ice and painting, writing, or performing. I watch a man in a gorilla suit and space helmet dance without any music. A woman wears a second body on top of her, the broken body her double, her doppelgänger, her past. Another woman undresses and poses inside the frame of a cube. She crouches inside the box until her feet bleed and someone brings her clothes. I feel so limited. All I have are lines for lullabies I could never sing to my son. I wish I had three orange cones and a knife. I could lie inside that triangle and ask someone to report the news of my death. Make it beautiful so people will want to hear it, make it sad so they remember, make everyone who hears about it want to deserve the life they've been given.

———

"In melody, as in sweet things, history's emotion finds refuge," Lorca said, "its permanent light free of dates and facts." I want that for my son. I want that for myself. A song free of April, of receipts, of knives between ribs. I want to unsee where my friend's body was recovered a month after he went missing—browning grasses, weary palms, a storage unit and two cranes in the distance, a gentle hill. The soil under him, rich. Around the star his body made, new shoots thriving.

Riddle at 29,000 Feet

You said marriage must sacrifice itself on the altar
of family, but this week I read about a man

who climbed back up Everest to find his missing wife.
I wash moonlight from your forehead and the Sphinx

in your chest asks again: *What comes down but never
goes up?* You never did learn how to waltz. The site

called Rainbow Valley earned its name from the bright
coats of all the climbers who never made it back

to base camp. The husband who went after his wife
is red is orange is blushing in the valley. Love is such

an unreliable savior. *What's so delicate that saying its name
breaks it?* The wife lived for two days in the cold. Saving her

was too risky, climbers said. Snow collected in her mouth.
The mountain whitened its history. She is blue is green

is singing when wind rides through her sockets. Who knows
if they had children. That's not the story. Ever, ever,

our happiness common, endurable. I ask what crazy thing
you'd do for me. Answer, the rain. Answer, silence.

Arctic Lullaby

Here in the not-night, there is danger

> in the zodiac, a stowaway on the ship,
> invisible mortal asleep below deck.

Little ghostling in your red box, refusing exit.

> Body all cell and ossifying bone. Long, beautiful it.
> Dear that. Darling this. Summer plus evening giants

means when you're born you must wander the below.

> The polar bear remembers what the snow forgets,
> but the terns are easy to please. Nestling, uncurl.

Fingerling, awake. Only snow buntings sing

> in the ever-day where light crusades from cliff
> to glacier and back. Here in the gray midnight,

you swell into being. Here of the bright lullabies

> and curtainless portholes, the narwhals migrating
> and old blubber ovens growing the greenest moss

in the archipelago. Little awe, lengthen. My petite seedling,

> nest of cells, abed in sweet and sorrow, building cardiac,
> nervous, respiratory. I, the holding and the holding back.

You, my soul doubling, the best terror I've known.

Dear Thanatos,

Goddamn the sweet ease of night.
Damn the daylight, too. Dream me.

Winter me. Sleep me somewhere numb.
Somewhere God doesn't summon me

from the side of a man who begs me to dive
the well and bring up the boat. I ate the liver

of a seal and a narwhal's arctic tongue. I shot
a humpback with a harpoon. It struggled,

but it sang the moral mysteries, moaned
its oral history to the submarines as it fell,

its body a hundred-year feast for the ocean floor,
the testament in its belly gone so wild,

so racked with doubt, not all the fat on
the whale's back could burn the meaning out.

Self-Portrait as Milk Hare in Active Shooter Alert

We plan our escape from the basement classroom,
students swapping memories of school shooter drills.
Trees blush and undress, though the scratching outside
our window is not the dead we fear to be. Today

in the news I read old stories collected by Irish children
of household medicine and hags who became rabbits
to lap milk from cows. I don't know why a witch would
need to, why she couldn't say *I'm a mother like you,* hold

her own cream in her cupped palm for the cow's rough
tongue, and ask for the kindness returned. The moon
occults the stars in Taurus, and my son performs sadness
over an otter that died at the zoo. He blinks slow and sniffles

back octaves of salt. I don't know where he learned this,
to be an understudy to the keening of trees planted too close
to houses. I read him *The Runaway Bunny,* say I would chase him
though all his transformations—be the gardener to his crocus,

the wind to his sailing ship, a tightrope walker when he learns
trapeze so we can both be creatures of air. One student says
Use me as a stool to climb from window well to lawn. I'm glad
someone wants to die for the rest of us. I don't want to give

my son a hero for a mother. I want to go home to him.
I want him to lose me after years of hugs, arguments,
and medically acceptable suffering, and I would take this
student's offering to leap from his back, like the milk hare

the farmer shot, then found his thieving neighbor in bed,
human again, holding her bleeding head. The farmer warned
her thirsty tongue, though he knew, as everyone did, that
bullets won't kill witches. I won't die for these students.

But I would draw on whiskers and pull myself from this
concrete burrow, dodge cracks in the air, aim for the gentle
corrections of trees' shadows. My body small enough for
hiding. My ears so large they can hear my name in my son's

prayer—red as the fear that will keep me on earth. Black
as blood in moonlight, in the fur that twitches back to skin
again, my son's arms safely around my neck, his milk teeth
and bubblegum cheeks breathing, breathing, oh, still alive.

Dear Eros,

You're not supposed to be here. You belong
in lower altitudes where air thickens with heat,
where your pleasures are ruthless and your words
are sweet. You accused me of hiding in beauty,
but what a breathless place to vanish, like this height,
this mountain, these snowdrifts named penitentes
for how they appear like ascetics on their knees.
I have asked my knees for so much. I asked a man
to hurt me like a professional. He asked if I liked pain
or humiliation more. How cruel to make me choose.
Darwin described these snowfields—with their tall
narrow peaks—as a crowd of penitents. I want to admire
the attitude of submission, but I want God's anger
more, want to rouse the Old Testament in me,

want to be both hand and cheek. Even when God
flooded the world, he loved it. Even when he promised
to destroy it again with cleansing fire. That's the way
I want to love. Soul, you raw little pea, there's nowhere
left to hide. Here at a border of Earth and atmosphere,
what you obscure with image reveals you, too. This isn't
prayer, it's what pleasure sounds like with two fingers
in your mouth. The fingers aren't yours, but the taste is.
I'd come here to look at the stars, but cones of snow
keep telling me to forgive, or to beg for it. There's no
escaping the desire to be unmade. Eroded. Even snow
knows it's unclean. Each flake makes its geometry
around dust, where everything begins. No one knows
why penitentes always face the sun, but I know why
I face it. To the man who told me, *Choose,* I said:
Call me what I am but hurt me, too. Let this pleasure be
a penance. I will suffer it again. Ask me to—

Dioskouroi

Once, twins cracked from a single egg, mortal
and immortal with the same spit curl

and troublesome Greek fate. Once, you and I
broke into the city garden. One broken gate,

two shadows over a fence. We left stones
in the birdless hands of Saint Francis

and our initials on the fountain. It's so easy to
forget when you're forgiven. And I did forget—

Jesus offers himself to whoever wants him,
shaving off flesh into every open mouth, and I

took it, stale and merciful, and forgot you at once.
Once I called, but the phone had been stolen

from your pocket. Once the wallet. Once a knife.
Once the fireless awe. The object is not objective.

I know the crime better than the criminals. Once
I scratched the scabs from your hands and called

them rubies. Faultless. Absolute. Once, when you
were living, I reddened my lips and powdered

my eyes as green as scarabs and tucked little liquor
bottles into my bra while you distracted the cashier.

That night we littered the beach with cheap plastic
and monologues on how art lets us live twice.

We believed it was good to live, better to remember,
best that memory is mapless. Once, one of the Greek

twins climbed a tree to escape his pursuer, but it's easier
to kill someone who won't run. I wish I'd told you

that story. Instead, I grew up, loved someone else,
I lit cigarettes to study the smoke and tattooed

your middle name on my wrist. Half an immortality
in serif. Trees blacker than their shadows.

Once I knew your body like Eve. Postlapsarian
but naked anyway. Your lower lip, a disobedience

and sweet. I meant to tell you, the other twin,
the immortal one, chose the fate of his brother.

They became stars and patron saints of horsemanship
and sailors. The night you died, I dreamed I was pregnant

and washed ashore clinging to the wooden breasts
of a ship's splintered figurehead. My eyes milky

with uninviting light. My back sunburned and peeling.
I birthed a two-headed horse. You baptized it. Once.

If That Mockingbird Don't Sing

I'll find you a bird with more admirable passions
and a syrinx made for nocturnes. And if its voice

can't soothe you, I'll find one of Sandman's disciples
in the foxglove. And if she offers to cast you

as King Arthur if only you'll audition in nothing
but chamomile and a sword, say yes—it's best

to stay on a dream-bringer's good side.
If all she offers is eternal sleep, say no,

but pocket the pill. God's only going to rapture
eleven souls, and sleep will be hard to find

after that. Who needs the ineffable when
you have sleep and the easy symbols of its saints?

And if dreams don't come to you with loose teeth
and shipwrecks and pirates in bikinis, I'll give you

a hand on your back and call your name, take you
from the dream against your will, and I will

give you the portrait of a nightingale grieving
like a gardener in winter. I'll give you a local God

and his raucous allegory. I'll diagram the moral
calculus of the fable and edit toward safety.

Beware the wolf always, but trust the witch
and the sugar crash. Not the star lore that

shadows your cheeks with your lashes. Never
the halo offered by the angel gowned in snow.

Dear Thanatos,

I did what you told me to,
wore antlers and the mask, danced
in the untilled field, but the promised

ladder never dropped from the sky.
In the burned house strays ate bats

on the attic floor, and trotted out
into the dark with wings in their mouths.
I found the wedding dress unharmed,

my baby teeth sewn to the cuff.
There's a deer in the woman, a moth

in the chimney, a mote in God's one good eye.
The fire is on the table now, the bear is in
the cradle now, and the baby is gone.

She's the box of bones under the bed,
the stitches in your lip, the moon and the hollow

in the geode, in peaches heavy with June.
If I enter the river I must learn how to swim.
If a wolf's ribs are bigger than a man's,

and if the dead float, then I am the witch's
second heart, and I am the sea in the boat.

Pastoral before Decomposition

I imagine it lovely, the place he was killed,
imagine darkness as clear as it was before God

learned to speak, imagine the Milky Way burning
through the light-stained night, imagine trees blacker

than the sky, and then imagine cicadas grating April.
The cold was crisp, I imagine, and scooped out stale

carbon dioxide from his lungs. One of those good pains.
My imagination wants to redeem the bareness of fact,

so I imagine the field he died in as a place we might
have picnicked, imagine wind entering his clothes

and leaving again—not the knife. No. I will only imagine
the way the cars versed themselves in curve and velocity

through the arterial streets. Not how the men took turns,
not the way his body proved to the medical examiner

that he struggled, lifted his hands to defend himself—
no, I imagine the grass, how it must have nodded along,

how his phone lit up with a blue light blinking, blinking
at the driver who stayed behind, his thumb brushing

the red END from the screen like wiping an eyelash
from his lover's cheek. I imagine her, only hours away,

letting the spring salt into her sleepless room, Atlantic
waves curling in on themselves, red tide creeping toward

shore, and the suffocated fish with bellies like moonlight
doing what is surely required of all the dead and rising.

Did He Who Made the Lamb Make Thee?

for P—, Q—, & K—

Did you drive past trees thriving in graveyards and think: *Holy, holy,*
Lord God Almighty? Can you forgive God for what he forgets?

Can you afford that kind of mercy? For he gave me the pleasures
of vendetta as he gave you shank, knife, machete, handsaw,
mile upon mile of good traffic and keys to a truck.

Did you imagine fingers could grow back like a starfish?
Did you give my friend a chance to run? Did you give him

the quickest death you could? God gave me twenty-four
days of false reports and candlelight vigils. He gave you
a new moon and two weeks in Miami. Did the crab legs

give you heartburn? Did the hotel sheets give off the smell
of bleach? How do you get blood out once the stain sets?

Ammonia? Salt? Soap and a good lather? Do you think God
will give you one last chance or say *Deep breath* to distract
you from the needle? Will he record your prayers and listen

later? What on earth will you ask for? What clemency? What
grace? How could you possibly believe it will be given?

Crime and Punishment

The night you died, I was alone and let the phone go
to voice mail. I ate from April's greening mouth,

oh, my sorrow. I did not know. No one knew. Who knows
why we were made in God's likeness but not liked by God.

At the prison art show, self-portraits by one of your killers.
He, the man weeping. He, the man caged. He, the matador

who caught the bulls' horns like a bouquet. He and I have
something in common after all. We beguile ourselves.

We dream of the same man after two glasses of moonshine.
Francis Bacon said a portrait teaches us about the artist,

in which case I am your killer's seceding heart with a torn
ventricle for a flag. The oldest recording isn't what I was told,

is not Edison shouting "Mary Had a Little Lamb" into tin.
It's a French folksinger ghosting "Clair de Lune" through

the scratching with news of moonlight. O starless, hereditary
night offended by facts. Who wants to hear the dead?

It's the dying I'm after. It's transformation that I want.
Even if I can't paint a smile or discreet red, I can practice

my injuries in private. I place your body in a field. I place it
in a closed casket. I place it in a paragraph. An image wounds

in the wrong location. The horror of a carcass is the beauty
of a butcher shop. I place your body in bed, a fan stirring

the hairs on your chest. At the prison art show, it all came out—
the undisciplined sympathy, the undammed need

of the condemned to speak as oil, as ink, as your death
tattooed on a stranger's cheek. The object is not objective,

but I always find myself on my knees in front of it,
choosing between God and all those lovely golden calves.

The brush herds the lamb into my hands and subjects it
to mercy. My pleasures are not accidents. I resurrected

the brazen bull's metal torso with watercolors, big enough
for a man, the tube from the bull's chest hollow so it can
transform the condemned man's screams into singing.
This is what I am waiting for, for the state to take

my revenge for me. I held a candle at the vigil, little thorn
of fire threatening to obscure what the darkness confirmed.

I want to see God's face, to lick the white of his eye, to order
him to die for me again. I want to dig up your body still clothed

in heaven and give you back to the world, give you back
as lightning, as the electric volt that rides through a man,

through the chair he's strapped to, his last words transcribed
for the record, known, remembered, unrightfully saved.

How to Sugar for the Atlas

Begin first with the intent to lure a bright species,
the luna with its lichen glow, or the cloudless sulphur
with its daffodil flutter. Ask the moon for the garnet
symmetry of the atlas with its wing powder like ash

or the wrong snow. Create the temptation—brown
sugar, stale beer, molasses, blackened bananas. Ratios
aren't important, but apply to bark with a paintbrush
while singing murder ballads until your trees reek

with sweetness. Coat them at dusk and wait for dark.
Watch for souls returning with furred faces and nocturnal
hungers approaching from arctic latitudes. Yes, call
his name when the first one arrives. Don't be surprised

he doesn't recognize you. Watch him dip his proboscis
with tender amnesia in the bait. Don't be surprised when you
need to keep him, this creature with spiracles that claims
not to know you. Bag and freeze him. Give him a gentle

second death, slow his panic to dull flaps. Help him relax
enough for saving. *This is another immortality,* you can say
as you pin and label him with careful ink. This is the kind
of cruel others will understand. You want him whole again,

not like his first death when police found him and thought
he was moving, how he looked dressed for the night before
flies rose from his body, holding the shape of him midair,
a shadow with a thousand wings, and then a prayer.

Murder Ballad in the Land of Nod

And Cain went out from the presence of the Lord,
and dwelt in the land of Nod.
Genesis 4:16

In a story with many firsts, the first man and the first woman committed the first sin and had two sons—one who offered fruit to God, one who offered blood in a garden. Somewhere east of Eden was a land waiting to receive exiled murderers. The Hebrew root of the word *Nod* is the verb "to wander." Cain left the still-warm body of his brother to enter a landscape made for a lifetime of lostness. But somewhere in Nod, he found a wife. He found her love, her comfort, the way she would kiss his eyelids to wake him in the morning. They had a son named Enoch and built a city in his name. Meanwhile, his brother's body was translated cell to soil to wild grass. All his sons were green and wandered until they covered the world.

———

The day the trial of my friend's murderers is scheduled to begin, it doesn't. There is no news about dates or justice or whether there will be one trial or three for the men who took part in his kidnapping and murder. The men have been waiting, not wandering. The defense lawyer pleads he is busy, overbooked. The judge says: *This is an old case. I know it's difficult to line up the sun and the moon and the stars.*

Everywhere the news repeats. The blond reporter separates her hands when she says *walking home* and connects them again when she says *fateful night*. Fate. Where does one go to meet it? . . . *body was found off the interstate*, she says, and the camera shows traffic, police officers, a field of saw grass. It shows the faces of the three men—the one who stayed in the car, the two who went into the field with my friend and returned without him. Three walked into the night. Two came back. Such awful math. So terribly simple.

———

The day the trial of my friend's murderers is scheduled to begin, there is news from the doctor that my blood could attack my unborn son. Usually this problem of blood is fine for firstborns, but I'd lied on my medical forms and said this was my first pregnancy. It was the first one I wanted. I mention that my medical chart may not be entirely accurate. I ask what I should do and am told: *It will probably be fine.*

I should probably tell the doctor the whole truth. I should probably pray. But what could I possibly say to a God who asked his son to die but let a murderer wander out of a garden, as if exile were punishment enough, as if mercy were that easy. *What is lost joins eternity. That's how the immortal maintains itself.* I find this written in an old notebook. It's my handwriting but the words seem to belong to someone who has only loved the living.

I spend most of the day in the nursery that's already finished. I read my unborn son the poem "Wynken, Blynken, and Nod," about three little fishermen rocked in a wooden shoe, casting their nets in the stars they mistake for herring. My son doesn't kick or turn or thump to the ABAB rhyme scheme, and I hope he's joined the trinity of sailors in sleep.

———

Sometimes I think about how much Cain's wife knew and when she knew it. When did he tell her about his idyllic home? When did he tell her about his brother's short life—sixteen verses between birth and murder? Did he tell her more than we know? We know field. She knew stone, or by his own hand, or a garrote made of wild grasses. We know he offered fruit; his brother offered a lamb. Did Cain say: *I gave God the thing itself and not the symbol.* Did he mean to say: *God wanted a blood sacrifice. That's exactly what he got.*

———

My friend was kidnapped in one county, killed in another, and the murderers were captured miles away from either. He was taken in a county named for a lion and killed in a county named for a saint—Saint John of Patmos lived in exile, banished for prophecy. I wonder if it's easier to have visions on an island—the livable environment surveyed and mapped, surrounded by the limitless ocean. John promised: *He thalassa ouk esti eti.* In the fulfillment of the messianic apocalypse, there will no longer be a sea. Once I was told that to escape from a desert island you should build a new boat out of the shipwreck, but what if instead of an island you are trapped in a truck with three men? What should you build then?

———

One of the murderers drew a sketch to help police find the body, hoping for a plea deal. He confessed the murder to another inmate, but the facts were wrong. Either he'd revised the truth of the events during his three years in prison, or he couldn't remember them anymore. He confessed to kidnapping my friend in the wrong location, murdering him in the wrong county with the wrong weapon, and claimed to have acted alone before driving to Miami. There he met a woman named Cheerie, but they had no sons and built no cities, and his wandering was over in a few weeks when the police broke down his motel door and found him with my missing friend's credit cards in his wallet and a bloody knife wrapped in receipts.

——

I wonder if Cain revised his sins as he lay in his wife's arms telling her the story of how his wandering began. Perhaps he told her he found his brother worshipping God in the wrong way, or claimed he caught him growing poppies among the figs or raising a mob of outraged angels to attack an intruder. Perhaps he remembered every blow he struck. Perhaps he remembered only his own fear and the blood on his hands and needed to invent the rest, to imagine himself a hero doing what he must to survive. In one version, he atones and God forgives him. In the story he tells on another day, he is cursed. I wonder if his wife wrapped her leg around his and felt something new to this world, a loosening of her heart akin to empathy, an amazement at her husband and his brother and all who've been made to suffer.

——

Where are you going, and what do you wish? the old moon asks Wynken, Blynken, and Nod. When the moon discovers the foolish fishermen are in the stars looking for herring, he laughs and sings, and rather than pointing them to an earthly sea, the old moon makes their mistake come true. All the burning stars they pull into their wooden boat are herring, and their boat becomes a trundle bed, and the three sailors become two closed eyes and a dreaming head. And those fish and that moon become a dream they can't quite recall upon waking, but they know they wandered far, that something wonderful and terrible happened, and they've returned with the stain of starlight on their palms.

From the age of thirteen, I had dreams about two men pursuing me. One was a man who loved me so much he wanted to invent a thousand cages in my honor. The other was a man who loved me so much he wanted to kill me—how else could I be his? They followed me for two decades on trains, across deserts, through forests, into the secret passages of old houses, and the one who wanted me dead always reached me first. When I got pregnant, I stopped dreaming about them. Now, I dream of leading a crusade of children over mountains, trying to find a safe place to open the Ark of the Covenant. I never tell them what we're carrying, and they follow me for the secret I keep from them. If they knew the truth, who knows what they would do, what they might become, how long they might pursue me to make me theirs alone.

While the trial is delayed, the prosecution says it will seek the death penalty. At first this horrifies me. Despite the Code of Hammurabi—*an eye for an eye*—that old wisdom that says vengeance is allowed and even necessary, I have long favored mercy. I believe in everyone's best self. And yet, when I see that my friend's family wants the death penalty, something deep and feral in me says: *Good.* My moral imagination fails. I do not care. Grief wakes the animal in me, and even though I know it is wrong, the anger feels powerful.

I discover that the death penalty in the state of Florida is by lethal injection, unless a convicted person chooses electrocution. So far, no one on death row has done so, but I am fascinated by the idea of this choice. I wonder if they offered my friend two ways to die, if they offered him a chance to pray, or a cigarette, or another cliché, if—worst of all—they offered him hope and told him to run into the wilderness.

Though no one knows for sure, some theologians believe that Lamech, Cain's great-great-grandson, murdered him. It's so appealing, this tidy closure. Revenge comes, though decades later, from a family member. Yet it still allows Cain years and years of marriage and children, the building of cities, drinking beer, telling stories, eating figs on the bank of a river, slaughtering lamb after lamb for the God that absolved him.

How could a mother know such a thing? How could Eve predict one son would kill another? Could Cain's wife know that the grandson of her son would kill her husband? They loved, they begat, they hoped for atonement. They prayed each day for natural deaths.

———

I read in the newspaper that pregnant women are genetic chimeras—they absorb part of their children's genomes. On autopsies of women who've had sons, the majority of them have Y chromosomes in their brains and breast tissue. *Thank God,* I say to my husband, knowing our son will always be with me. My husband points out that because my blood believes our son's body is an invading organism, it will probably reject any fetal cells he leaves behind. The shots I receive hide the traces of my son from my immune system so my body won't learn he's not a part of me. I wait for him to be strong enough to arrive, full of terror and godless breath.

———

My husband says I must stop anticipating terrible things. But terrible things happen all the time. Maybe if I imagine the worst one more time I will find the scenario that saves my life or someone else's. Two men will walk with me into a field, and we will all walk out. We will come slumberless to the Land of Nod and await the slow arrival of forgiveness—blood evanescing from their hands, my heart accepting the clean sadness of grief, God's indifferent kiss insulting each of our wounds with its cure.

When I imagine my friend's death, I try not to think of the hours he spent in the truck afraid, watching the mile markers, thankful, perhaps, for each minute, each humid breath. I try not to think about what he might've said to the men who, perhaps, hadn't decided whether they would kill him. Or maybe they always knew how it would end, and so did my friend, but he told them things about himself anyway, to make himself real. I try not to think about what he must have thought, whom he might have wished to call. When I imagine his death, he walks through the field and doesn't feel the men like twin shadows at his back. He recognizes a constellation. He feels the earth give a little with each step. He thinks the word *help,* and something does.

Second-Born Lullaby

Perhaps I just need the old-fashioned terror
      and awe of the Old Testament metaphors—
Absalom hoisted into the tree
      by his own beautiful, betraying hair;
Job's dead children an exposition
      for the spectacle of his suffering;
Isaac laid out on the rock as sacrifice,
      as symbol, as a boy trembling
at God's will and his father's willingness.
      Rock-a-bye, child, the world is fucked,
but that's been true for millennia;
      why give up our grim inheritance
for a miniseries on ghosts? How
      could moths eating through the slip
inside a wedding dress rival Jezebel
      the moment before the first dog bit?
How could the corpses of foxes howling
      through a hole in the stomach of a girl
being whipped by a man with a flaming
      mustache compete with Patmos? The terror
of a true god burning all others at the stake.
      I am too much, it's true. Perhaps
I should see the dead serpent in my garden
      as a milk snake surprised by a lawn mower
and not a stand-in for evil or desire, but
      every image is merely the domestic understudy
to stories we inherit. I want a bird in my hair
      like a vision, want manna in my hands
like an answer. I want to lay my son down
      and say, *The darkness in me is not*
the darkness in you. I want to say, *God loves you*
      like a father. I want to believe it.

Vive, Vive

Last night, I slipped my finger in the milkweed,
my hand doing the wind's work. It was so soft,
that crooked slit aching open but not far enough
for those white tufts to float away. I couldn't help
myself. And I didn't want to. I wanted to tease out
those stubborn seeds and make them leave as
they're meant to. Stupid little futures hiding from flight.
A friend tells me she had a dream about me holding
an armful of apples in a treeless field. *Write a poem
about it,* she says. *Call it "Come What May."* I want
to call it "My Joys Are Selfish Whores" and suck
the worm from a Red Delicious. But wasn't I good once?
Didn't I play penitent with a floral sheet bobby-pinned
to my girlish curls as I rocked the doll's plastic lips
to my flat chest and called it the Lord's? What now?
Lowly animal, I've pitied myself like any mammal
that hurts. I've described the papillae on a cat's tongue
to my son, how the wet sandpaper that cleans
our salty fingers is a predator's tenderness,
the tongue evolving into a tool to lick bones clean.

None of my prayers are questions anymore.
Just aching stanzas full of chrysanthemums dying
on the kitchen table. At our anniversary dinner,
my husband and I agreed we wouldn't talk about
pain—no new medications, no dosages, no metaphors
for what's failing in his body now, or how this
new pill will make him die for trying not to suffer.
He had the pork, I had the balsamic-glazed duck.
There was apple torte and coffee at the end. The sun
set. We said nothing. There was no language without
sorrow in it. That terrible near-symmetry. I set out
my nativity two months early. I always confuse Joseph
with the shepherds, but there's no mistaking Mary
and her silent baby, staring up at the bored sheep.

I paint her robe with nail polish called Starter Wife.
My Lord, why is goodness so hard for me?

I lick a battery to feel a spark before putting it
in the toy ambulance. *Dead,* I think, my tongue
unjolted. At least now I won't have to hear the sirens
wailing their false emergencies after my son loads
the swaddled baby Jesus in the back. My husband
is in his room again, where he goes to be alone
with his suffering. I think of my wedding. Of the sky
that day. The hope I had. The shame of it now.

Our old cat paws at the back door, hissing at something
beyond the gate, growling at what only he can see
in the dark. I hiss at him. I want him to know danger
is coming from both sides. You can't even trust what you love.
He claws at the glass anyway, as if there were any fight left
in him, as if this meanness isn't what we all do when
we know how helpless we are. God, God, what do I do
after all this survival? Another friend dreamed of me saying,
I can't bear it anymore, and sprouting glass feathers from
my shoulders and arms. She said the dream wasn't windy
but they fluttered as if they weren't glass. Even in dreams
I'm flightless, incapable of escaping. My prayers return
as a knife and the commandment I carve into the skin
of an apple, gentle with the flesh, gentler with the blade,
before I suck the sweetness from each of the wounds I made.

Dear Eros,

He was always a wingèd thing and I was always
a grave, an openness. That's how we knew
our belonging and how we knew it wouldn't last.
I was too bloodless, staining our garage with new
prayers of anger and broken coffee cups. The homes
we made in each other gave us bouquets torn from
spring branches, four walls we mortgaged, and dishes
shaking in their cupboards. We used to walk
the arboretum and subtract ducklings each week
without any grief. The old celery fields smelled
of cinnamon some days. Others, mint. I'd jump
on his back as if we were young, nearly innocent,

with laughs as dark as our halos. I wished *Always*
but the dandelion seeds were stubborn, everything
ripe refused my mouth. When I said *Come home,*
it was a lie, but I believed it. For a year I was light
shaking on the surface of the water, a fire softening
into a flood, and once his hand around my arm
like a snake circling a branch in Eden. Not all secrets
are shames, and this one isn't either. It's the pale
green of healing. It's my lips opening like parentheses
and his name inside, it's turning back from the wrong
north, the moon like a slice of raw onion, my skin
weeping like a fever, closing the question with my hand
around my other arm so I'll match, so I'll burn.

Oh Wonder

It's the garden spider who eats her mistakes
at the end of day so she can billow in the lung
of night, dangling from an insecure branch

or caught on the coral spur of a dove's foot,
and sleep, her spinnerets trailing radials like
ungathered hair. It's a million-pound cumulus.

It's the troposphere, holding it, miraculous. It's
a mammatus rolling her weight through dusk
waiting to unhook and shake free the hail.

Sometimes it's so ordinary it escapes your notice—
pothos reaching for windows, ease of an avocado
slipping its skin. A porcelain boy with lampblack

eyes told me most mammals have the same average
number of heartbeats in a lifetime. It is the mouse
engine that hums too hot to last. It is the blue whale's

slow electricity—six pumps per minute is the way
to live centuries. I think it's also the hummingbird
I saw in a video, lifted off a cement floor by firefighters

and fed sugar water until she was again a tempest.
It wasn't when my mother lay on the garage floor
and my brother lifted her while I tried to shout louder

than her sobs. But it was her heart, a washable ink.
It was her dark's genius, how it moaned slow enough
to outlive her. It is the orca who pushes her dead calf

a thousand miles before she drops it or it falls apart.
And it is also when she plays with her pod the day
after. It is the night my son tugs at his pajama

collar and cries: *The sad is so big I can't get it all out,*
and I behold him, astonished, his sadness as clean
and abundant as spring. His thunder-heart, a marvel

I refuse to invade with empathy. And outside, clouds
groan like gods, a garden spider consumes her home.
It's knowing she can weave it tomorrow between

citrus leaves and earth. It's her chamberless heart
cleaving the length of her body. It is lifting my son
into my lap to witness the birth of his grieving.

Dear Thanatos,

Last week a pregnant woman ate rat poison at dusk
and feared the light she woke to.

The last time I stood in front of a mirror, a monster
crawled out, forlorn and flailing, who looked like my mother
when she dreamed of snakes.

I bit its neck until it stopped moving, split it open,
and where its first heart should be, I found a model of the moon.

I never consented to this. The telescope lens cracked.
I can't see the Pleiades.

This week, an auction house found a copy of Milton's *Paradise Lost*
bound in the skin of a convicted murderer—

a ratcatcher by trade who poisoned his lover with roasted apples
and milk, whose flesh now clothes a book about temptation
and the architecture of hell.

Mine is a thrifty grief. It recycles its nails.

When I broke open the cupboard, I found the monster's second
heart made of blank paper and burning.

Sleep Regression Lullaby

No matter, the moon will anoint its other princes,
and you will remain Lord of Thwarted Sleep.

Your body with its endless appetite for stars and milk.
My body with its groggy offering. When you were born,

my sister said, *Maybe now you'll write some happy poems.*
But she's a mother. She should know better. Two by two,

dreams confirm their alibis, but you prowl painted blocks
with sleepless intent. So I try to sing you something happy,

like balloons rounding the corners of your room, like daffodils
who refuse to know the season and thrust through December

frost, like my mother's letter when you were nothing
but a few cells, how she said it was God who was making you,

knitting you whole. Perfect, her faith that the unseen
would prove its love through you. Enough. This night calls

for stronger magic, a song rigged for sleep, and so I'll sing you
something I'd never dare say—some nights I switch off

the headlights and count to ten, some nights I get the urge
to eat you and bite your cheeks. My sister reached into

our dead mother's mouth to tug her tongue. *Just to make sure,*
she said, and I thought *Sure,* like praying even though

no one answers, how even if you pulled out his bloodless
tongue, God still wouldn't know which mother was yours.

Fledgling

I scare away rabbits stripping the strawberries
in the garden, ripened ovaries reddening
their mouths. You take down the hanging basket
and show it to our son—a nest, secret as a heart,
throbbing between flowers. *Look, but don't touch,*
you instruct our son, who has already begun
to reach for the black globes of a new bird's eyes,
wanting to touch the world. To know it.
Disappointed, you say: *Common house finch,*
as if even banal miracles aren't still pink
and blind and heaving with life. When the cat
your ex-wife gave you died, I was grateful.
I'd never seen a man grieve like that
for an animal. I held you like a victory,
embarrassed and relieved that this was how
you loved. To the bone of you. To the meat.
And we want the stricken pleasure of intimacy,
so we risk it. We do. Every day we take down
the basket and prove it to our son. Just look
at its rawness, its tenderness, it's almost flying.

Mystery, Play

Rather than the miracles, one-acts of all the failures—
      Sampson's pillow talk, Cain sacrificing a still life of pomegranates,
            Sarah offering Hagar as a gift to her husband,

Hagar unable to refuse. I left the religion, but kept the sin
      and its images. Keep catching snakes and feeding them apples on stage.
            After intermission, God's more recent debacles—

tsunamis, polar bears, the nurse who said my mother could
      go home, the doctor who misread her chart, the dream in which
            my mother pins herself to the mattress

with hypodermic needles in her wrists—painless, forsaken,
      overprepared for namelessness. Her suffering transformed
            no one, least of all herself.

On a scale of 1 to 10, the pain dissolves like a Eucharist.
      God always meant to watch his son die. Sweet Jesus, love child
            of history and deserts. Mother-Christ

and her dead-end ascendance, nursing that hope of heaven
      on her dead breast. On a scale of bearable to feral, I am raised
            by wolves and showing. When God's

courage failed, Mary watched. Centurions with nail guns.
      Monotone heartline. Homely spirit slipping out, whole as an egg.
            Right hand of God bleeding like a lamb.

Lullaby at 102°

Let the moth muster some enthusiasm
    for the streetlight. Let the tap run cold.

Let the laundry lie limp on the line. Let indigo
    bruise the hillside. Let dust-stung and withered.

Let wind be the reason. Let July. Let clouds marshal
    over the stars. Let the night be good.

Let the dreams be merciful and full of snow.
    Let rain. Let rain. Let the lilies close if they can.

And let thunder arrive with rattles and drums
    and aspens lashing the windows. Let lightning

find the tallest spear of grass. The fire that burns
    the sheets casts such easy and welcoming light.

Dear Eros,

I did this to myself, I know. You are not mine
but come as wind clotted with the end of a season.
Did you know all a ginkgo's leaves fall on the same day?
Sometimes it's called maidenhair. For its beauty.
For how easily it quakes. Of course you know,
you expert on falling. Did you know a friend told me
that the first thing he learned in a rescue class was how
to break the arm of the person he was trying to save?
But what if this time the only person I want to save
is myself? I would ask what I have to break, but I know.
My therapist: *You're resilient. You don't just survive trauma;
you thrive in it.* Did you know the ginkgo excels at healing
itself? Surely you who made yourself in the image of
a Madonna with a glacial face and a bloody fist in
the chest know what it means to make your heart
an ocean. Mine is greedy, weak. In my best moments,
it might be Lake Eyre, flooded for six months with useless
abundance, dry the rest. But not you, not your stubborn

metaphor. Thank you for that combustible muscle—
I mean that—it can't be easy to open both sides of a robe
and bear that much tenderness for strangers. To accept
so much terrible need. I've done it, though. You know
I sat naked next to electric heaters in dusty classrooms
while the circle around me attempted my widening hips
and unclenched hands in charcoal. I even kept a sketch
to remember myself young, nearly pretty, a perfect
subject who didn't mind vulnerability and stillness until
the timer chimed. When someone offered to hurt me
any way I wanted, I put their hand around my throat.
That time, choosing it. Where do you keep your secrets?
I know. The bottom of your vestments where the blue
takes over. That purple pulp of you finds spark and oxygen
and convinces everyone you've given all you have, but
you're holding back. We all do. I can be as impatient
as any ginkgo in October, but I can hold my hand over
the back burner, low heat, burn colder, oh watch me bear it,
watch me break, wait for the robe to drop from my shoulder.

Somnambulant

A lucifer hummingbird drinks the light ripening
on the prudish oleander tattooed on my shoulder
A windup nightingale sings to its open cage
and Jesus's scabs   redden like parables
A parade of my mother's nightgowns reciting the last
Please she ever wept as I roll them   off the roof
Everything takes back its comfort except the waning
in my blood   There's waking to be done post-solstice
Ghosts climb trees to watch me save myself
from another fire I started   I keep surviving the night
Stillness the same as dreaming   My nightgown sudden
with rhinestones   The quiet in me hears a hymn
written on God's tongue   North, the oldest glow
South   the gospel dark   black bells chiming *Stay alive*

Dear Thanatos,

You caught me by the wrists in the art museum.

I wanted to desecrate that godforsaken row
of disfigured saints with their fondness for the sky
and their wounds opening like little doors to heaven.

If I'd had spray paint, I would've used it.

If there'd been a wasp dizzily circling the Messiah,
I would have crushed its humming body
into the Lord's forehead, stinger and all.

I sang to the museum guard until he let me

babysit the angel. I pulled out all my teeth so it knew
I would not fight back. I was tired of surviving.
My heart had outgrown me. It wanted too much love,

too much sadness, too many arrows and glasses of wine.

But the truth is that the angel died as it seized my arm,
and I could not break its fingers. That thumping
you hear is not my pulse leaping but bones

knocking on the city streets as I drag the angel home.

Murder Ballad Awaiting Sentencing

Some people weren't meant to survive this life.
MY MOTHER

On the day I bury my mother, I check the news for updates. The last of my friend's three murderers is found guilty. The jury recommends death. The other two men have been sentenced to lethal injection. The judge has five weeks until sentencing. Five weeks to decide if this last man should live or die. The men who killed my friend spent three hours deciding whether to kill him—the problem of the robbery-turned-kidnapping solved in three hours in a deserted stretch by the freeway. Though perhaps they never debated it at all. Perhaps they were only waiting for the right stretch of road, the right field, with grass tall enough to hide a body.

———

My son can't sleep. Or I should say my son can't sleep peacefully. He rolls and thrashes and wakes himself crying. I worry that it's nightmares, that he can tell something is wrong, can smell my dead mother on the sheets. In "On Lullabies," Federico García Lorca claimed: "The child comprehends much more than we think. He is in an inaccessible poetic world, that neither rhetoric, nor imagination the procuress, nor fantasy can penetrate; a flat plain, its nerve centers exposed, of horror and keen beauty, where a snow-white horse, half nickel, half smoke, falls, suddenly injured, with a swarm of bees furiously nailed to its eyes." But my Internet searches assure me his fitful rest is not the nightmarish Lorcan bees humming in his skull, but is a common phenomenon in infants called *sleep regression*—he is suffering from difficulty adjusting to his sleep cycle and startles himself during light sleep. It's not the nightmares that are the problem—he can stay in those and stay asleep—it's when he drifts too close to wakefulness that he startles and cries. Advice columnists say I must wait it out, do what works to help him sleep. The only thing that soothes him is when I grab both his hands in mine and pin his body to my chest. Immobile, he can sleep. Restrained, he is peaceful.

Instead of helping my sister plan our mother's funeral, I stay up in my mother's room with my son, bouncing, rocking, singing, trying to keep my voice monotonous and sweet. Waiting song by song for his eyelids to drop and his breathing to slow. I try a version of a lullaby my mother taught me. Always my arms full of his uneasy weight. My mother's old song. My voice off-key. My son frightfully alive.

———

His death was not a gentle one, the medical examiner tells the court. This is when I should have stopped reading the news report. It should have been enough to know the trial had finally ended. Soon, something resembling justice might be served, or the forgiveness I was waiting to feel would loosen my heart. Either way, at least it would be over. That knowledge should have sufficed, but I read on, needing to know. Did my imagination come close to the truth? Can the imagination ever accomplish that?

I finally get my son to take a nap in a hammock by the pond. The ducks here in Florida have monstrous heads, red and knobbed, as if they've survived a scalding. Pushing the ground with my toe to keep us rocking, I scroll through the story, careful to keep my movements small. My sister is busy making a collage of photographs of my mother. My brother and his wife are on the front porch, keeping their griefs to themselves. I am hiding in an older death to keep from facing a new one.

The medical examiner in my friend's case came out of retirement to examine what remained, his knowledge specialized, necessary. There's no rest for someone who knows what he knows. So when the remains were finally found, he looked at this young man's body in the advanced stages of decomposition to discover what he suffered and where.

———

We order an autopsy for my mother. We do not know why she died, the weeks in and out of the ER, the vomiting, the weakness, the tests all inconclusive. We'd grown accustomed to the panic. The emergency room became routine. Send flowers. Send a card. Assume the mystery would leave her body again so she could come home.

The afternoon she died, nurses had told my brother she could probably be released that day. It was sunny. Warm. I walked my son through a parking lot and thought, *My mom is going to die soon.* But the world seemed so indifferent, I couldn't imagine it was true. These are the details that I knew—that calmness, that assurance, those thoughtless robins, that bored sky. Then, the seizure. Then, code blue. Then, my sister on the phone saying, *They lost her,* and for a second I think the nurses wheeled her into a hallway they've forgotten, and they need us to come down and search.

We won't get the autopsy report for a month, but when we do, it contains the weight and color of her organs. Her body eased open, each part examined and replaced, each part perfect except the heart.

———

It gets better when I stop blaming myself. I tell myself it's not my job to get my son to sleep. It's his job to get himself to sleep; it's my job to make sure he knows he is loved, is safe. It does get easier. It's just time. I whisper, I kiss, I cradle. I wait. Lorca, so full of promises: "Unlike us, the child possesses his creative faith intact and is still free as yet of the destructive seed of reason. He is innocent and, so wise. He understands, more deeply than us, the ineffable key to poetic substance." I imagine the lullaby my son would write if he could. Something bloodless. Something with milk and a mother's sweet sweat. Something that ends with light and an instinct to drink from the body you're held to.

———

Before the funeral, the pastor we hired says we must not make a spectacle of our grief. We must celebrate her life, limit the length of time we talk so that there's enough time for his sermon on Lazarus. *Fuck these men of God,* I think, talking about somebody pulled back from the brink of the light, who got to embrace his sisters again. What a terrible choice of material for a group of grievers, this man with his second chance. Heaven has never seemed more ridiculous.

    None of my sadness feels real, only my anger. My son cries, and my husband takes him away so I can be by my mother before they close the casket. Her pink sweater hiding the autopsy incisions stitched shut, the trace of the mortician's hands soothing the embalming fluid through her body, massaging her limbs to break the rigor mortis and make sure the fluid runs all the way to her fingertips. Her hands still too stiff, her face too slack, her hair refusing to curl around her ear no matter how many times I push it there. The roses on her grave ache open for days.

———

I try everything—lavender baby shampoo, mechanical heartbeats, a plastic turtle with constellations punched into his shell. I sing. I rock. I wait for the nights to pass, for my son's troubled sleep to turn restful and deep, but my son and I are awake for the new phase of the moon. The sleep regression doesn't pass. Lorca makes new promises for a new kind of lullaby in which mother and child go off to sleep together, that comforting unit of *we:* "Danger is near. We must shrink, be small, so the walls of the little hut brush against our bodies."

Lullaby one. Lullaby two, naming the parts of his body to a melody. Two eyes, two ears, two lips, a nose. Two arms, two legs, ten tiny little toes. Night-light on, I read him stories featuring a cat, an owl, a runcible spoon, and one about a toadstool circle, a changeling, the woods lacking even the mercy of a wolf.

———

The catalogue of damage to my friend's body:

Skull fracture

Stab wounds (multiple, repeated, also in the skull)

Broken ribs

Broken forearm

Severed finger

———

Does it help to know that after a certain threshold the body doesn't feel any more pain? my husband asks. *At a certain point, the brain can't even process it.* How could it help? To know that my friend's body was taken to a point where it could feel no more than it already felt. Is it a comfort to know my mom did not have a chance to cry out, to broadcast the pain that swept her away so quickly? What kind of balm is that? Who does that soothe?

I know nothing of that kind of pain, though when I scroll through headlines looking for solutions to my son's sleep, I find an article that says sleep depravation "is less overtly violent than cutting off someone's finger, but it can be far more damaging and painful if pushed to extremes." I imagine the nights with my son as if they were a walk into a dark field, and all that could happen there, but they're not the same. Pain and pain+fear are different kinds of suffering. Motherhood is pain+joy. My sleeplessness is love+delirium. All my pains these days are small ones, inconveniences—hangnail, headache, my tender gums bleeding on the white flesh of the apple.

———

Cause of death: homicidal violence.

The verdict: guilty.

The judge returns. Everyone rises. The third and last man who helped murder my friend waits with his head down, looking at his hands and listening. He is given life.

You Said the Lambs Were Ready

Aim behind the ear. Point-blank is a mercy.
If this were sacred, we'd let it run freely as it died.

But we are part-time believers and tie the legs. I fold
your recipe for mint jelly into the crane's blue paper.

A group of geese is only a gaggle on the ground.
In flight, they become a skein. A lamb is a lamb

is innocence turning into meat. But this was always
your DIY heaven, twenty acres of making a go of it.

A group of cranes is a siege or a mobile for a nursery.
Circular flight without ambition or stratosphere.

We hang the body from the swing set and set out
a bucket for blood. You ask me to get on my knees

with such tenderness. To adore what is above you, sublime.
To adore what's beneath you, we forgo the soft-core

pleasures of narrative. I swear I prayed to feel only good
desires, but the "I" in every new poem is Judas or Eve.

I used to leave notes under your windshield wipers that said
A group of solitudes is a family. Now you ask me to leave

addresses so you'll know where to start looking. Absence
as evidence, as timeline. I want to believe my heart is better

than its choices. I rub the lamb's ear between thumb
and finger before I pinch it and whisper, *Do it, fool. Run.*

Things That Will Not Appear in This Lullaby—

This cast-iron cradle on an overburdened bough.
That stone doll with a quartz heart and agates for eyes.
A boy waving a red skirt at a girl pawing the street in patent leather shoes.
The pirate ship circled by a shark that feeds on moonlight.
Mermaids training with tridents.
Instead, I'll sing about Cain seeing his shadow and crawling
        back to his den for a longer winter.
Your father, his sweater held open like a sling weighted with pears.
Your father, anointing my wrist with a paper corsage.
My love, the fourth-longest river in the world.
Someone else's love, between the road and the woods.
Not bells. Not God. Not snow. Not Nod.
Not Job's first loss, or his forty-eighth, but his wife swaddling the second
        set of sons she'd been given to replace the ones taken.
Neither never, nor Neverland, but always and here.

Family Portrait as Denouement

The night the mother forgets to call and the father thinks,
She's dead, and I'm stuck raising our son alone.

The night the son says he can't sleep because moonlight
rashes the curtains, and the mother thinks, *Dear God,*

don't let him be like me, always awed by the suffering of others
in a way that is half empathy, half desire, the way she dreams

of catching white rabbits by their ears and touching the pink
jelly of their eyes with more curiosity than tenderness.

The morning the father says, *I understand now why people stay
together for their kids,* and the mother thinks this must be how

much he loves their son. Must be. What else could he mean?
The father thinks he lost something, but he has his keys,

his glasses, all socks in their pairs tucked neatly together.
And the mother thinks of how much gas is in the car,

how far away she could get before stopping. And the son
wants to know if the coldness circumnavigating his heart

is called God, but before his parents can enter the room,
white petals disappear into his shadow like a conclusion.

Dear Thanatos,

It wasn't a dream. I gave birth to a one-eyed angel.
His placenta was a fig slick with honey, so I ate it.
I nursed him with grapes crushed between my breasts.
What can kill you is sacred, so my child was sacred,
blond and vengeful. His ribs said, *Enter me,* and my shadow
said, *Yes.* He took the silver coins hidden in my mouth
and laid me in the tall grass. The stars said, *Where am I?*
My dress said, *Rip.* I saw no clouds but I saw the wind,
who only wanted a daughter, and I had none to give.
There was the black tongue sliding deeper into the earth.
There was his one good eye—open, silvered, my initials
carved in the center. So little in me wanted to live.
The darkness said, *You die whether you risk anything or not.*
I emptied ashes from my pockets. I crawled to feel
the stones cut my knees, God's foot on my throat.
The dream said, *Follow me.* The angel said, *You're here.*

Dear Eros,

I asked my son which part of his body he loved most.
He said his skeleton. I always used to think I loved
my feet, a quarter of my bones splayed into fans,
the nerves so bright and easy to please. A friend's daughter
showed me the bones she'd filed in an old card catalog.
I handed each one back, the dull heat of rot traded
for the glare-white of a bare rib, fleshless cradle of hip,
heft of femur on a mantel. She and I shared our love
of lemons, and she taught me *witch* in her made-up language
so I could call myself by the proper word. The invented one.
I held myself against the hard belly of those vowels,
that black glyph of a name. The pulse I once felt
when my son turned inside me thrummed against my hand.

Tonight, the splinter I let live in my thumb finally worked
its way out of my flesh, the wound larger than the weapon.
I asked my son which part of his life he loved most.
He said crying. Because it felt so good to stop
when he was happy again. The daughter shows me
the thin hair of roots whitening the soil in a jar.
She has made this small wilderness and given it life.
When my marriage was failing, I offered to take care
of my friend's succulent. It was almost winter. Everything
was going gray. So when the plant began to bloom,
I welcomed its dusty pollen until the kitchen smelled
like carrion and bone dust. The house grew heavy with need,
with an ache I understood. The smell of death was simple
to answer. I knew what those fetid yellow stars required.
I opened the back door to invite the flies to their desire.

If That Diamond Ring Don't Shine

Well then, rubies or topaz or a star sapphire
gleaming from a witch's middle finger,

but not the finger itself, which I will hide,
just the gem and the gold it glimmers from.

And if that pulls you from your doze,
then Brahms, or its sequel with a brighter budget

and computer-simulated roses. If not milk,
patience. And if not patience, we'll hunt

the mockingbird and all his known aliases. If not
the shepherd's roll call of onesheep, twosheep,

three, then we'll listen to the secular gossip
of cicadas, who have only one rumor anyway.

If not the documentary on the nocturnal habits
of Serengeti predators, then the outtakes.

If not nannied by stars or nursed by the moon,
then dreams that don't know your middle kingdom,

your vowel dominion, your stage-one REM cycle,
your hypnic myoclonia, your stir and hush and cry.

Sphinx

The last night you slept in our house I saw a sphinx
moth ruining herself on the moon's reflection.
Darling metaphor at my feet. Damn fool. The water

in me reached out for itself, which is the way of all
good mirrors. It wanted its nest of stone. An hour
before we'd scratched our ceiling into snow, dusted

the blanket fort where we held each other and did
the quiet work of goodbye and then the siren work
of pleasure as the sheets fell down around us. I felt

the dark coin of blood wish itself onto white cotton.
I hadn't known the meaning of missing, though lost
was always clear. I gave your ghost ten minutes

to ache in me. It took my throat. I took the wings
from the moth. They were the soft, dishonest
brown of my eyes. They wanted to belong to me.

You must remember, though you weren't there.
It was the night you said sloth was not a vice
of laziness but the refusal to seek God. The moth's

furred body twitched in my palm, drew her legs
closer. My hands, an unclosed envelope,
a failed prayer. She'd spent herself on the image

of her desire, bright as a communion plate.
When I left her wingless body on the wet moon
I wanted her alive. I envied her suffering,

thought she got what she wanted—not longing,
not regret, but fulfillment, a whole sky,
nothing in the end but light flooding into her.

Thanatopsis

It's hard to believe, I know, but I swear most elephants weigh
less than the tongue of a blue whale. This might be easier

to believe: I dream of dead lovers when my anxiety is high,
their lashes like parentheses, their amputated histories

thickening in me like bezoars when I lick the little black mouths
of the shower drain. When I practice my new lover's death,

I judge my love's depth by how many tears arrive for grief's
rehearsal. I've practiced card tricks, crossovers, quick comebacks.

When Dalí heard rumors Lorca would be assassinated, he painted
a piano floating out of a skeleton's teeth. Can you believe it?

Can you believe a hippo can open its mouth wide enough to fit
a four-foot child inside? I keep forcing my child still against a wall,

balancing a pen on top of his skull to measure if he's past the point
he would fit in a dangerous yawn. A woman tells me her husband

committed suicide last year with the gun she helped him buy
fifteen years ago for that purpose. A relief, I think, to not imagine

every death but wait for the one you know is coming. She has
a new hip, she says, an acheless steel joint. Maybe she'll even

dance again, her hair red as desert light and survival. It's also
hard to believe, but right now vibrating honeybees are

cooking a wasp with the heat of their bodies. I've imagined
my son dead. Imagined his loss in summer cars, in sleep, from

an unholstered hero on a playground. Already he tells me he will
love me even when I'm dead. You think I should only believe

what I see, but I test my hand in a cardinal's nest and hear its
wingless heat, and I see a skull's smile slide toward music resting,

unplayed, above it. Can't you see it? My son's ribs, a white
hive, a prolific darkness. My love can't save him. Unbelievable.

The body, an instrument. Goodnight, a warning. His mouth
falls open so large in sleep I can see the future swarming.

Dear Thanatos,

Not, I'll not kiss your lionlimb, not lap back the rattle in my ribs
        like a lone pill going to powder

in an orange plastic bottle. Not, no, not sing anymore of the wretch
        and wrestle. No more ministers

to drive words through my wrists and leave me for the patient circles
        of scavengers. No. You didn't kill me.

Not because, some days—yes—I wished for it but chose a different
        courage. I stopped asking the mirror

for a dream and opening it like a door. I wished to welcome back
        feeling, that whole mansion of trembling

rooms, wished to break every window, let the light storm through.
        On my knees I wished for tempest,

for rack and screw. I asked for churchless pleasures to disturb
        my numb comfort, wanted lick

and wallow, wished to swallow the laugh out of my child's mouth,
        and—my God—wished

for even the shame of an apple. Now my wishes are down to two:
        Staying alive. And wanting to.

From the Buried Kingdom of Together Still

Let's not call it *denial* anymore
Let me name the miles between his mouth and mine Temporary
      as Season   and then let it be spring and bruiseless again
rank as geraniums in the noon heat
astonished as skin before blood slips like a memory
      across the distance of a wound

Like you I have let myself belong to someone
and stood on a bridge and told him I'd never leave
two days before I did
                But who doesn't offer
      a lie when the air heaves, unsweet and green,
with a stalled rain and a sky blue as a new world

Let's not call it *bargaining* anymore
and say a wish is the daughter of longing
Natural Consequence   Youngest Shame   Oldest Hunger

Let me come to the altar of each noun and offer

      to *distance,* burnt roses and a western wind
      to *time,* the black hourglass in the gold of a goat's eye
      to *greed,* my tongue, rotten garnets scabbed at its root

But not my vocal cords, the pearl of each blister hurting its sister
      the sternum-burn of that scream   its painful goodness

When you tell me I held the ashen love of a marriage
and accepted its death   but my husband kept trying to resuscitate it
      I put a cigarette out on an apple
      bend it into an italic *S* in the skin
                  I bite the flesh
where I burned it   taste the pink-and-gray wind of April
when Kansas ranchers drip torch the prairie

Maybe when I said *always* I meant
asleep like honey   new as a crocus   as far from now
as the ghost that sank between us like a promise or a knife

Let's call it *then* or *never* or accept that a heart heals
          like a grave
                              Let the bluestem and switchgrass insist
until I call myself A Thousand Yeses   until it is true

Contender

It's alright to overdress for the riot. Your rage is stunning.
It's alright to pursue the wrong pleasures and the right suffering.
Here's my permission. Take it. It's alright to replace a siren

with a bell. Your emergency should make its music. It's alright
that the meter reader broke your sunflower in half. You knew
better than to plant it where you did. Sometimes it's alright

if you call your waiter *honey* when you order sweet tea. It's alright
if you fall out of love with being alive, but rise again tomorrow
with French pop songs and fresh croissants, wear all your gold

to church, and try—really try—to believe anything but a stethoscope
can hear your heart's urgency. It's alright that your mother died.
So will your father. And your son. But hopefully not before you.

It's alright to lie naked in the rain and refuse to go inside even
when the moon tries to make your cold thighs shine. It's okay
to lick the ice-cream cake from your fingers. Do it. Now. In front

of everyone. And if what falls on the children lining up their cars
for the soapbox derby is not snow but ash, that's alright. Celebrate
the mutable body. And if you write notes to friends and senators

in primary colors, that's fine. It's even okay to begrudge the stubborn
pears in the wooden bowl. You're right, you know. They're waiting
to yellow until you turn away. It's alright that in the economy

of forgiveness you keep coming up one daffodil short. It's alright
if you ask your heart to grow the size of Secretariat's—not because
you want to outrun other horses or because your legs are classic

but because you, too, want to be buried whole after someone
examines the insensible engine you left behind—iamb of the
beloved's name no longer metronoming the valves—and places

that slick fist in a stainless tray for weighing and shouts *Sweet Jesus* before describing its ungodly heft with superlatives, your heart the most tireless, wildest, wiliest, thirstiest heat on record.

Dear Eros,

You say Eden disappeared   open the book and read
but the sea   which no one tends   is also a garden

Our prayers rise   wingless and nighted by frost
The angel's fossil burns like alcohol   across the mouth

of a wound   Forget the dull evangelical vision   Heaven
still springs and fruits   beneath the fathoms

The snowflake eel caught in a birdcage   You're safe enough
to surrender   to my hand up your shirt   my tongue

on your ear   Our hearts gold as honey   turned to crystals
inside the harpooned cachalot   It's fine if you're ribbed

with echoes and nets   For too long I stayed   an untended bed
of starfish   Now I follow the coven of thunderheads

I don't want suffering   to offer its thesis   I want out
of exile   and back to a garden where we can confuse

innocence with goodness   I want the christening of thunder
My love witches a second chance   from the bottom of the sea

I believe in the way ice heals itself   in the way a fish accepts
the lesson of the hook   Take your mouth off

my breast   the world isn't there   So much forgiveness
awaits us   the green seas part as the angel approaches

Notes

"Did He Who Made the Lamb Make Thee?" takes its title from William Blake's "The Tyger."

"Crime and Punishment" is after Francis Bacon.

For Lamech in "Murder Ballad in the Land of Nod," a good source is Robert Alter's *Five Books of Moses* (W.W. Norton, 2008).

"On Lullabies" by Federico García Lorca, translated by A.S. Kline, was used in the essays "Murder Ballad in the Land of Nod" and "Murder Ballad Awaiting Sentencing." https://www.poetryintranslation.com/PITBR/Spanish/Lullabies.php.

In "Second-Born Lullaby" the lines "corpses of foxes howling / through a hole in the stomach of a girl / being whipped by a man with a flaming / mustache" are from Mark Halliday's review of *Our Lady of the Ruins.*

In "Murder Ballad Awaiting Sentencing," the article quoted is "Why Sleep Deprivation Is Torture" by Kelly Bulkeley in *Psychology Today,* Dec. 15, 2014. https://www.psychologytoday.com/us/blog/dreaming-in-the-digital-age/201412/why-sleep-deprivation-is-torture.

"Thanatopsis" is after Aimee Nezhukumatathil's "Dream Caused by the Flight of a Bee Around a Pomegranate One Second before Waking Up."

"Dear Thanatos, [Not, I'll not kiss . . .]" is after Gerard Manley Hopkins's "Carrion Comfort."

"From the Buried Kingdom of Together Still" is after Natalie Diaz's "From the Desire Field."

In "Dear Eros, [You say Eden disappeared . . .]," the italicized line is from William Carlos Williams's "Asphodel, That Greeny Flower."

In several poems, I quote friends. They are: Maia Carlson, Lisa Fay Coutley, Minadora Macheret, Jim McLachlan, and Jennifer K. Sweeney. A special thanks to Lulie, who gave me the word *witch* in her made-up language. I won't tell anyone the real word. I swear. And to Elliot, whose words appear here so often: I love you beyond reason, and I hope nothing I have shared hurts you later. I still have so much to learn about forgiveness.

About the Author

Traci Brimhall is the author of *Saudade* (Copper Canyon Press), *Our Lady of the Ruins* (W.W. Norton), winner of the Barnard Women Poets Prize, and *Rookery* (Southern Illinois University Press), winner of the Crab Orchard Series in Poetry First Book Award. Her poems have appeared in *The Believer, Best American Poetry* (2013 and 2014), *The Nation, The New Yorker, Orion, Ploughshares,* and *Poetry.* She has received fellowships from the Wisconsin Institute for Creative Writing and the National Endowment for the Arts. She's an associate professor of creative writing at Kansas State University and lives in Manhattan, Kansas.

Poetry is vital to language and living. Since 1972, Copper Canyon Press has published extraordinary poetry from around the world to engage the imaginations and intellects of readers, writers, booksellers, librarians, teachers, students, and donors.

WE ARE GRATEFUL FOR THE MAJOR SUPPORT PROVIDED BY:

THE PAUL G. ALLEN
FAMILY FOUNDATION

Anonymous
Jill Baker and Jeffrey Bishop
Anne and Geoffrey Barker
Donna and Matthew Bellew
Diana Broze
John R. Cahill
The Beatrice R. and Joseph A. Coleman Foundation Inc.
The Currie Family Fund
Laurie and Oskar Eustis
Saramel and Austin Evans
Mimi Gardner Gates
Gull Industries Inc. on behalf of William True
The Trust of Warren A. Gummow
Carolyn and Robert Hedin
Phil Kovacevich and Eric Wechsler
Lakeside Industries Inc.
on behalf of Jeanne Marie Lee
Maureen Lee and Mark Busto
Peter Lewis

TO LEARN MORE ABOUT UNDERWRITING
COPPER CANYON PRESS TITLES,
PLEASE CALL 360-385-4925 EXT. 103

WE ARE GRATEFUL FOR THE MAJOR SUPPORT PROVIDED BY:

Ellie Mathews and Carl Youngmann as The North Press

Larry Mawby

Hank Meijer

Jack Nicholson

Petunia Charitable Fund and adviser Elizabeth Hebert

Gay Phinny

Suzie Rapp and Mark Hamilton

Adam and Lynn Rauch

Emily and Dan Raymond

Jill and Bill Ruckelshaus

Cynthia Sears

Kim and Jeff Seely

Dan Waggoner

Randy and Joanie Woods

Barbara and Charles Wright

Caleb Young as C. Young Creative

The dedicated interns and faithful volunteers
of Copper Canyon Press

The Chinese character for poetry is made up
of two parts: "word" and "temple."
It also serves as pressmark for
Copper Canyon Press.

This book is set in Granjon LT Std.
Book design by Gopa & Ted2, Inc.
Printed on archival-quality paper.